Take A Backyard Bird Walk

By Jane Kirkland
with
Rob Kirkland
Dorothy Burke
Melanie Palaisa

Ready?

You're about to set out on a real adventure. Not only will you make discoveries and see things you haven't noticed before, you're going to help complete this unfinished book, and only you can finish it!

Here's an example of a bird walk adventure. One summer day, I was walking to my mailbox at the end of my driveway. As I passed through the garage door I saw a bird fly out of a nearby pine tree. I decided to look in the tree to see if the bird had a nest. What a surprise I found!

There were four baby mockingbirds in the nest waiting for food from their mother. I ran back to the house to get my camera, took this picture, and wrote about it in my journal.

You can find birds any time of the year and almost any time of the day, but the best time for a bird walk is in the early morning or late afternoon. This is when birds usually feed, and you will see them flying around looking for food. You'll make new discoveries each time you take a backyard bird walk.

Are you ready to make a discovery like this?

What is a Backyard Bird Walk?

A backyard bird walk is an adventure you take to find and identify the birds in your backyard. You can walk alone or with your friends, brothers or sisters, parents, or even the whole family! You can also take a backyard bird walk in your schoolyard with your schoolmates or while you are away on vacation.

Don't Have a Backyard?

Backyards come in different shapes and sizes, and some people don't have a backyard at all! If you don't have a backyard, take this walk in a local park, around your apartment complex, in a schoolyard or at a friend's backyard.

Set?

For your bird walk you need this book and a pencil or pen. And why not bring along a trash bag? You can put any trash you find in it and help keep the environment clean for all its inhabitants — even yourself!

Complete as little or as much of this book on your walk as you want. You can carry the book again and again and complete a little more of it each time you take a bird walk.

What should you do if it's raining or the weather is bad? Well, you can have fun watching the birds from your window. As soon as the weather is better, go outside to complete your walk.

Here are some of the things you will do on your bird walk:

✓ Take field notes to help you remember your walk, including information about the weather and all the birds you see.

✓ Draw a map and sketch the path you take so that on your next bird walk, you can remember where you saw birds.

✓ Draw pictures or take photos of the birds you see.

✓ Write down questions or thoughts you have about birds and other discoveries you make on your walk.

✓ Identify the birds you find, and learn interesting facts about the birds commonly found in your backyard.

✓ Write a story about your exciting adventure.

Here's an Idea

Do you know someone who might enjoy taking a bird walk with you but who can't come along? Perhaps your grandparents can't get around very well, or maybe you know someone who is ill or disabled. They can enjoy your walk if you share your book with them and your stories about the discoveries you made.

What to Wear

Your walk can be as short as 15 minutes or as long as several hours. People say "*Time flies when you're having fun,*" and time will fly when you take this bird walk! So remember to protect your skin from the damaging rays of the sun and also to protect yourself from biting insects.

If you take a bird walk in the winter when it's very cold, be sure to bundle up in layers of warm clothes and to wear shoes or boots that will keep your feet warm and dry. If it's raining, don't forget to wear your raincoat.

Go!

What are Field Notes?

Scientists, artists, and naturalists often take notes called "field notes" when doing research or while making observations. When they write down information in their field notes, they are making a record of such things as the date, the weather, and what they see.

Keep the field notes you take on your first bird walk. When you take another bird walk, you can compare your old field notes with the new ones. You might discover that you saw certain birds on one walk and different ones on another. Your field notes might help you to learn why. For example, it could be because you took your walks in different seasons or at different times of day.

Got a Twitch?

People all over the world watch birds and they have done so for centuries. On a trip to England I visited with some backyard birdwatchers—Mr. and Mrs. Hughes and Mr. and Mrs. Brunning. Birdwatchers in England use some very different terms than birdwatchers in the U.S. For example, they call their bird feeders "tables" and they call their backyards "gardens." Birdwatchers are called "twitchers" and if you go out looking for birds you are "going on the twitch." I wonder what your parents would say if you asked them if you could "go on the twitch!"

Take this book and go outside to your backyard. Stand very still for a moment while you look at and listen to what's going on around you. Let your eyes scan the ground, the sky, the rooftops, and any trees, bushes or fences you see. Listen carefully. Do you see or hear a bird—or several birds? Do you see or hear other kinds of creatures like humans or dogs or even bees? If you have a bird feeder, do you see or hear squirrels? Squirrels are always near my bird feeder!

When I feed the birds I end up feeding the squirrels, too. This one is raiding the seed I placed on a table for the birds.

After you get a good look around, draw a map of your backyard (or wherever it is that you are taking this walk). If you're not artistic, draw boxes and circles to represent the things you see. Label your boxes with descriptions such as "house," "pine trees," "playground," and so forth. Add to this map every time you take a backyard bird walk and you'll know where to find the birds and their nests.

When you finish your map, begin your field notes.

My Map

What to Draw:

Whether you're in a park, your backyard or a schoolyard, here are items you may want to include in your map:

☐ Trees or groups of trees and bushes.

☐ Bird feeders, birdhouses and birdbaths.

☐ Flower gardens or food gardens.

☐ Patios, decks, and fences.

☐ Paths, sidewalks, buildings and parking lots.

☐ Playground equipment.

☐ Lakes, rivers, creeks, or swimming pools.

Need more room to draw or write? Use blank paper or download free forms at www.takeawalk.com.

Go! 5

My Field Notes

Write This

Your field notes should contain information specific to this day and this bird walk. For example, write about the weather. Is the sun shining? Is the sky cloudy? Is it raining? If there is snow, write down how deep it is. Record the season and the current temperature if you know it.

You can also use this page to make a list of the birds you see during this walk.

Write what you can now. You can write more during or after your walk.

Need more room to draw or write? Use blank paper or download free forms at www.takeawalk.com.

What Are Birds, Anyway?

Birds are animals with wings. They can fly. They build nests and lay eggs in the nests. Do you agree? But lots of other animals can do those things. Bats have wings and they fly. Alligators build nests and lay eggs. Bugs fly. But none of these are birds. Besides, some birds—like ostriches—don't fly! Other birds—like the brown-headed cowbird—don't build nests. In fact, the brown-headed cowbird lays one egg each in the nests of other birds. When the cowbird egg hatches, the bird that built the nest feeds the baby cowbird along with her own babies.

A brown-headed cowbird is not a flying cow!

Some species of birds live in one area all year long. Other species go south for the winter and return in the spring. They migrate. Some travel as many as 20,000 miles a year! Scientists believe that birds use the sun and stars (as well as landmarks) to navigate from one location to another. Many birds migrate at night. Birds migrate to follow their food source. During winter there are species that migrate _from_ your area and species that migrate _to_ your area. Where are the insects in the winter?

Now, this is a brown-headed cowbird.

So, what is unique about birds? Feathers and hollow bones, among other things. No other animals have feathers. And the birds' hollow bones make it easier for them to fly because hollow bones are lighter than solid bones. Some scientists believe that birds are descended from dinosaurs—did you know that?

See All That You Can See

With binoculars, you can get a close-up view of the birds and their homes. If your parents or older brothers or sisters have a pair of binoculars, ask if you can use them for your walk—don't borrow them without permission. Ask someone to teach you how to use the binoculars, and always hang the binoculars around your neck from their strap. Most binoculars are expensive, so don't ever carry them in your hands, as they can be bumped or dropped. Binocular repairs can be expensive, too. Once, when I was in my canoe, I dropped a pair of binoculars in the lake because I didn't have the strap around my neck. And those binoculars didn't float!

Matt and His Grandfather

Our readers often share their backyard bird walk stories with us. Matt Kravitz (age 11) wrote this:

"My grandfather and I took binoculars down to a creek near his house. He showed me how to focus and use the binoculars. We found about 10 different kinds of birds including a Pileated Woodpecker and another very large bird that we didn't recognize. He has lots of books about birds so we wrote down the features of the bird and went home to try to identify it. We had a lot of fun doing this."

New Word?

Predator (PRED-a-tore)

An animal that hunts other animals, intending to kill and eat them.

Leave Only Footprints

When you take a walk, remember to leave only footprints! In other words, don't drop trash where you go, and watch where you walk so you don't step on any flowers, garden plants, or small animals. If you're walking in a forest or park, don't move the stones and logs—these actions disturb little animals' homes.

Some birds will come very close to you if you are quiet and patient. One winter day while walking through the woods, I found a tree stump where someone had placed seed for the birds. Chickadees were flying to the stump to eat the seed. I picked up a handful of seeds to offer to the birds. I called to them by whispering "psht, psht, psht." Before long, two and three birds at a time were eating from my hand! Chickadees are especially friendly little birds. Perhaps you can try this in your own backyard.

To see birds up close, you'll need to walk quietly and slowly. Most backyard birds are used to some noises around them, such as the noise made by traffic or humans or squirrels. You'll find that the birds will tolerate some noise from you, even your voice if you speak softly.

But quick movements and sudden loud noises can startle birds. It's my impression that birds don't like it when you stare at them. Many *predators* will take the time

I provide mealworms for the bluebirds in my backyard. It took a lot of patience and a lot of time before the birds trusted me enough to eat from my hand.

to study their prey (the animals they will kill to eat) before they attack, and I figure the birds think I'm planning to eat them if they see me staring at them!

Sometimes, I sit very still on my deck near my bird feeders for long periods of time with food in my hand for the birds. Over time the birds in my backyard have gotten used to my presence and some birds will now eat from my hand, like the Eastern Bluebird shown in this picture.

New Words?

Habitat (HAB-i-tat)

Where one lives. A bird's or animal's habitat is the part of the environment in which it normally lives.

Territorial (tair-a-TORY-el)

To claim an area as one's own, keeping others out.

Species (SPEE-shees):

A certain kind, variety or type of living creature.

Which birds you see depends upon the **habitat** in your backyard or on your bird walk. Some birds like open ground, others like trees, and many like shrubs and brush. Birds you see during spring and fall might just be stopping by during migration. Even these birds are looking for their favorite habitat.

For example, you won't see birds normally found in lakes and ponds if you don't have water nearby. If you do see ducks, geese, herons or shorebirds, there might be water nearby. Of the birds that live near or on the water, there are some that like salt water and some that like fresh water. Maybe you have a swimming pool. I once saw mallard ducks swimming in my neighbor's pool.

This bird plans to migrate the easy way!

If there are a lot of trees or bushes in your area, you will see birds that nest there, like catbirds or mockingbirds. You might also see birds that eat bugs (such as woodpeckers) or nectar from flowers (such as hummingbirds).

Some birds are **territorial**. Territorial birds don't allow other birds of their **species** to live nearby during nesting season. You might see a flock of bluebirds in the winter but in spring you might see only two because they've chased away all the others from their nesting territory.

A Famous Birdwatcher

John James Audubon (1785—1851) is the world's best-known painter of birds. During the 19th century he wandered all over North America, painting pictures of every species of bird that he could. Although other people also painted pictures of birds, Audubon was the first to depict them in their natural settings, acting as they naturally did. He published his bird paintings in a series of books, called **Birds of America.**

One version of this book, the Royal Octavo edition, became the first popular bird *field guide* in American homes.

Audubon also studied the behavior of birds, and published his findings in a book called **Ornithological Biography.**

New Word?

Nocturnal (noc-TURN-al):

Active at night, sleeping during the day. Opposite of diurnal (Die-URN-al), which means active during the day, sleeping at night. Which are you?

Sing Like a Songbird?

Did you know that some songbirds don't sing? And some songbirds mimic (imitate) the songs of other songbirds. A robin's song is pretty and most people recognize a robin when they see or hear it. But when is a robin not a robin? When a mockingbird is imitating a robin's song!

Some bird songs you might recognize are: blue jays, crows, cardinals, robins and mockingbirds. Many of the birds in your backyard are songbirds.

Speaking of songs, do you know any songs about birds or any songs that have bird names in them, like *bluebird* or *eagle*? If you do, why not try singing softly while you walk? Perhaps if you sing, the birds will sing, too. Who knows?

You might see birds of prey, like hawks or falcons, if you live near a field, because fields are good places for them to find mice and other yummy food to eat. You might also see a vulture in the sky. Many people think that a vulture is a bird of prey, but it's not. Vultures are scavengers. They eat what's already dead—like road kill (yuck). Birds of prey hunt living things like mice or other small mammals. Be sure to look high in the sky where birds could be soaring. One time I saw a bald eagle flying above the grocery store. Can you imagine that?

Claire Weber (age 15) drew this barn owl and the hitch-hiking bird on the preceding page. I love her artwork!

Can you think of any birds of prey that I haven't mentioned yet? How about owls? Of course! But many owls are *nocturnal*, so odds are you won't see them during the day.

I bet most of the birds you see today are songbirds. Songbirds are part of the bird family *Passerine* (PASS-uh-reen). Eighty percent of passerines are songbirds. Passerines live in almost every kind of environment. What sets a songbird apart from other passerines? Among other things, its voice box. Songbirds have more muscles controlling their voice boxes than other birds. That's why they can sing prettier songs!

An American Goldfinch is a songbird. It's also a backyard bird that visits bird feeders. Goldfinches can be found in all parts of the U.S., but they usually like to go to the northern states during the summer. Have you ever seen an American Goldfinch in your backyard?

Which Birds Do You Know?

There may be many birds that you recognize right now in your backyard. Maybe you already know what a robin or a mockingbird looks like. Make a list of the birds you know. You can come back and add to this list later if you remember more.

There are hundreds of species of birds in North America. In this book we discuss the smaller, more common birds you might find at your feeder or nesting nearby your house, such as songbirds. Later, we'll show you some birds that may be new to you.

List The Birds You Know

Harry and Mr. Owl

One fall evening my friend Harry went on a nature hike at a local park. The park ranger tried to attract a screech owl by playing a tape recording of its call. But the tape recorder didn't work, so the park ranger tried whistling like a screech owl instead. He must not have been very good, because no owls answered his calls.

Later that evening Harry stood in his own back yard. Wondering if any owls lived in his neighborhood, Harry tried to whistle the way the ranger did. Within minutes, a small screech owl swooped at Harry. It passed so close, Harry had to duck, and his hair fluttered in the breeze created by the owl's wings. Harry never heard the owl approaching, it flew so silently. Then the owl perched in the maple tree and watched Harry.

These days Harry calls his friend "Mr. Owl." Every night Harry whistles and Mr. Owl comes right away to say hello.

You, too, can learn to talk with nature. But first you must listen. Listen to how our feathered friends sound, and then practice whistling just like the birds do. Before long you too may be chatting with your new, feathered friends. Early some evening, if you whistle just right, Harry's friend Mr. Owl might fly by and say hello to you.

New Word?

Juvenile (JEW-ven-nul)
Not fully developed. Not yet an adult.

Lauren and Her Blue Friend

Our friend Lauren Frail (age 11) wrote this great story about her backyard bird walk:

"I thought the brilliant colors of the birds that I saw were great. I was looking through binoculars and guess what I saw? A blue jay glided off a tree in such a way it almost looked like he was falling, but just when he was about to fall onto the ground he swooped up. What a show-off!"

A Book for You

This is one of my favorite books. I think you'll enjoy it. It's the true story of a little bird that preferred the company of humans to other birds. Robert became a very famous bird!

That Quail, Robert, written by Margaret A. Stanger, published by Perennial Publishing.

Field marks are the features of a bird that can tell us its species and sometimes its age and sex. In other words, field marks help us to identify what kind of bird we are looking at.

When you see a bird, you might be able to identify it from a picture in this book. If you can't find your bird in this book, write down a description so you can look it up later in a field guide that lists all the birds. Write down as much information as you can about the bird. The next few pages will help you decide what to look for and what to write down.

This American Goldfinch will help you to learn the parts of a bird and field marks that are useful when you are trying to identify a bird. When you see a bird, first look at his color and the color on the wings, breast and other parts. Keep in mind that some birds have different colors in different seasons. Males and females of the same species may look different from each other; and *juvenile* birds often look different from adults.

As you study a bird, you can pretend you are an ornithologist (or-ni-THOL-o-gist). That's a scientist who studies birds.

Identifying Birds

Here's a checklist of observations you should make when you see a bird:

✓ **The size and shape of the bird.** You can't really measure a bird when you see it, but you can compare its size to a bird you know. For example, a robin is 10 inches long. So is your bird bigger, smaller, or the same size as a robin? Is it shaped like a robin, or is it shaped more like a dove or a hawk?

✓ **The bird's bill.** The shape of the bill helps you to determine what the bird eats and which family he belongs to. A finch has a different bill than a wood-pecker.

✓ **The overall color of the bird.** Color is an important key to identifying a bird. Look for the overall color of the bird and then, as the goldfinch picture on page 12 showed you, look at the colors of the bird's wings, breast, head, eyes, tail, face, legs, feet, and so forth.

✓ **The location of the bird.** Where do you see this bird and what is the bird doing? Is it on the ground eating, on a tree branch flicking its wings, flying from flower to flower, or hanging out at your bird feeder? This information is very helpful. For example, robins don't usually visit bird feeders, so if a robin-sized bird is at your feeder, it's probably something other than a robin. Robins don't usually climb up tree trunks, so if you see a robin-sized bird climbing up the trunk of a tree, it's probably not a robin, but it might be a woodpecker.

✓ **The bird's song.** If you can hear the bird and remember his song, this is very helpful in identifying the bird. I can tell you, though, that bird songs can be difficult to remember and, well, there are entire books written about bird songs. But if you work at it, you can identify birds by their songs.

Do Birds Affect Your Life?

For me, birdwatching is an enjoyable and relaxing hobby. I like to imagine what it must be like to be a bird and fly around. I like to watch the birds communicate with their songs and their body movements, and I wonder what they are saying to each other.

Birds come in lots of sizes and colors, just like people! Birds carry seeds so plants will grow, and they help to control the insect population. Birds also provide food—do you eat chicken or turkey? How about eggs?

How do birds affect your life? Do you ever wonder what it would be like to be a bird? Can you imagine life without TV, computers, or ice cream, and no place to come in from the rain or cold?

Can't Find Any Birds?

Before you can identify the species of a bird, you must find a bird. If you haven't seen one yet, look a little harder. Try looking in these places:

✓ On the wing—which means the bird is flying.

✓ On the ground.

✓ In trees and bushes.

✓ On man-made structures like buildings and telephone wires.

✓ At the bird feeder or birdbath.

If you don't see any feeder birds or song birds, look around for a predator such as a cat or a hawk. These predators will keep the birds away. Wait until the hawk leaves or put the cat in the house (if it's yours). Try looking for birds again about 15 minutes after the predator is gone from the area.

Laura Lists Her Birds:

Laura Ann Habina (age 9) wrote this about her backyard bird walk:

"I saw a robin, American Goldfinch, a bluebird, a blue jay, a cardinal and a Northern Oriole. I hope to see some of these birds again! I wish I had seen a Black-capped Chickadee because it is small, plump, high-energy and cute! They eat insects, seeds, and berries. They live in wooded areas of almost any kind."

No, only adult male cardinals are red. In many bird species, the males are more colorful than the females. Male birds are brightly colored to attract the females. Females are less colorful so as not to attract predators to the nest.

The American Goldfinch is another species in which the males are more colorful than the females. In addition, the colors of the male goldfinch are more intense during the breeding season than in the winter, when he is much duller and not the pretty bright yellow you see here.

Goldfinches live in farm areas, open areas with shrubs and trees, and suburban yards and gardens. The adults eat seed and feed their young by eating first, then vomiting into the nestling's mouth. Most other songbirds feed insects to their young.

A juvenile male goldfinch looks like an adult female until he grows into his adult colors. The same is true of the cardinal. Some birds take a long time to mature and grow into their adult colors. Did you know that it takes four to five years before a bald eagle has a white tail and head? And have you ever noticed that some gulls are brown? Those are the juveniles.

Northern Cardinals (8½") are found in the eastern U.S. as far west as Texas and Mexico. They live in shrubs near open areas, in the woods, and in suburban yards.

The American Goldfinches (5") shown here are in full breeding colors. See the brightly colored males? One of their favorite seeds is thistle seed. American Goldfinches can be found in most of the U.S. and southern Canada.

What's in a Bill?

A bird's bill is an indicator of what the bird eats. Some bills are made to catch insects, some for sucking nectar, and others for cracking seeds or opening pinecones to get at the seeds inside. Other bills are strong enough to cut or tear through meat. The bill is also used to preen (clean and smooth their feathers), and it can reach almost all parts of a bird's body.

Here are some common songbird bills (or beaks). The birds you see in your backyard may have one of these types of bills.

Seed

Here you see a cone-shaped bill (#1) and a crossbill (#2). Cone-shaped bills are good for cracking seeds. Birds with crossbills insert their bills into pinecones to get at the pinecone seeds.

Insects

A thin, long bill (#3) is good for picking insects off of leaves, twigs and bark. A strong, tapered, chiseled bill (#4) is good for pecking holes in trees to look for insects.

Live Prey

A sharp, curved bill is used to bite the skull or neck (ouch!) or to tear meat (#5). A bill with "teeth" (#6) on the side is used to cut through food.

Nectar

A needle-like bill (#7) is good for inserting into flowers to get at the nectar.

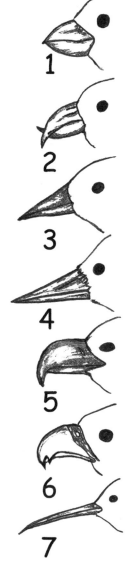

Websites to Visit

Visit these Websites for more information about birds and birdwatching.

audubon.org

This site shows you how to make your backyard bird-friendly, how to make watchlist trading cards, and how to help our environment.

pbs.org/lifeofbirds

This is the companion site to David Attenborough's PBS series "Life of Birds." Read about bird brains, bird evolution, bird songs, and parenting. This site also has links to other bird-related Websites.

naturesound.com

Here you will find pictures of songbirds and you can listen to bird songs.

Keyword Searches

To find Websites about birds try searching using the following keywords:
ornithology
birds
birdwatching
kids and birdwatching

You can also search specific names of birds, such as:

bluebird

robin

Bald Eagle

woodpecker

A Book for the Whole Family

There's no doubt that you really need a good field guide to be a birdwatcher. But how do you know where to go when you want to see birds other than the ones in your backyard? Try this book:

Seasonal Guide to the Natural Year (Fulcrum Publishing)

This book should be a part of every family's collection! It's a month-by-month guide to the natural events in your area. It's not just about birds. It's where I look when I want to take a spring drive to see wildflowers or I want to know where and when to go whale-watching. It's also where I learned that just 50 miles from my house I can see thousands and thousands of snow geese and tundra swans in one place during spring migration.

There's a Seasonal Guide to the Natural Year for almost every region in the U.S. They are written by different authors (both the Mid-Atlantic and New England Regions are written by Scott Weidensaul). To find this book, search for the title at your favorite online bookseller or inquire at your local bookstore for the guide that covers your area.

In between backyard bird walks why not take a family drive to explore nature beyond your backyard?

A bird with a bill made for eating insects doesn't necessarily eat only insects. When I put peanuts in my feeders, insect eaters—like woodpeckers, nut-hatches and jays—enjoy them very much! Here are a few close-ups of different kinds of bills.

This female house finch has a short, stubby bill great for cracking open the shells of seeds. One of her favorites is sunflower seed.

This White-Breasted Nuthatch has a bill made for digging insects out of tree bark. He likes to work his way down the tree trunk, head-down just like he is on this feeder.

The American kestrel has a bill made for tearing meat. He eats large insects, mice and small birds.

There is one other observation to make when watching birds—what does the bird look like when it is flying? Some birds flap their wings often when they fly; others soar. For example, you can identify a turkey vulture by its distinctive flight pattern. The turkey vulture holds its wings in a shallow "V" shape and rocks from side to side as it soars. I've noticed that downy woodpeckers dip up and down when they fly and eastern bluebirds fly in a straighter line. Watch a bird's flight pattern and write it down. Your notes might help you later when you are trying to identify the bird.

Recording Your Observations

How many birds did you know and list on page 11? If you knew six different kinds of birds before you started reading this book, that's pretty good! Have you seen birds today that you can't identify?

Let's observe some of the birds you saw but didn't recognize. Use the Bird Notes on the following pages to describe those birds. You can list up to two birds on each sheet. If a bird stays around long enough, sketch it on your page. You don't have to be an artist to sketch the bird, and your drawing will be helpful later when you are trying to identify the bird.

After you record some observations, you can look for your bird on the Bird ID pages that follow. It's very possible you'll see birds not mentioned on the ID pages. A field guide to birds will help you to identify the birds you don't find here. If you don't have a field guide you can check one out from your local library or your school library, or you can purchase one at an online bookseller or your favorite bookstore or nature store.

Field Guides for You

A field guide will help you to identify all the birds you find in your backyard. Listed here are three field guides I recommend. Look through them at your local bookstore and choose the one you like best. Each of these books covers the birds of North America (unless the book has an eastern and western version) and each has a different look and feel. Personally, I like them all, but you only need one!

Focus Guide to Birds of North America written by Kenn Kaufman, published by Houghton Mifflin. Digitally-enhanced photographs of birds make this one of the best field guides for North American birds. This book covers what it says—all the birds of North America in full color photographs. Get this if you plan to travel from your region so you don't need an eastern and western book.

Peterson Field Guides to Birds written by Roger Tory Peterson, published by Houghton Mifflin. Color illustrations, available in eastern and western regions.

Stokes Field Guide to Birds written by Donald and Lillian Stokes, published by Little, Brown. Color photographs, available in eastern and western regions. This guide provides information about feeding, nesting and behavior patterns of birds as well as their population trends.

How to Use

I filled in this sheet so you can see how to use the form. I took a picture of one of my birds and I sketched the other. The bluebird was with his parents, which helped me to identify him.

New Word?

Mottled (MOT-tld)

Covered with multi-colored spots or streaks.

	Bird #1	Bird #2
Location of bird	On birdbath	In bushes
Overall colors	Dark Gray with white spots and some blue	Brown
Wing bars (yes or no)	No	Couldn't see
Color of wing bars	None	None
Color on head	Blue	Brown with white eyestripe
Color on chest	Mottled gray/black and white	Buff
Color on Back	Blue, grey and white spots	Brown
Other physical characteristics	White eye ring, blue wing tips	Short tail, bobbing up and down
Approximate size and shape	About 7" shaped like a robin	Smaller than the bluebird
Behavior notes	Begging for food from parents	Loud 3 syllable call
Identification?	Eastern Bluebird (juvenile)	Carolina Wren

Use this area to draw or paste a photo of the bird

Bird Notes

	Bird #1	Bird #2
Location of bird		
Overall colors		
Wing bars (yes or no)		
Color of wing bars		
Color on head		
Color on chest		
Color on Back		
Other physical characteristics		
Approximate size and shape		
Behavior notes		
Identification?		

Use this area to draw or paste a photo of the bird

For You

There are lots of books about birds for kids. Here's one you might enjoy:

Backyard Bird Watching for Kids written by George H. Harrison, published by Willow Creek Press. This book covers the better known backyard birds. It recommends plants for the birds, gives ideas on how to feed birds, and teaches you about birdhouses to build or buy.

Need more room to draw or write? Use blank paper or download free forms at www.takeawalk.com.

Go! 19

Bird Notes

Julia Sings Like a Bird:

Ten-year old Julia Patterson wrote this in her Backyard Bird Walk book:

"I found there are more birds than you think. They all make different sounds, and sometimes you can sound like them and they answer you back."

	Bird #1	Bird #2
Location of bird		
Overall colors		
Wing bars (yes or no)		
Color of wing bars		
Color on head		
Color on chest		
Color on Back		
Other physical characteristics		
Approximate size and shape		
Behavior notes		
Identification?		

Use this area to draw or paste a photo of the bird

Need more room to draw or write? Use blank paper or download free forms at www.takeawalk.com.

Identifying Feeder Birds

A "feeder bird" is a name used for the many species of birds that are likely to come to your bird feeders. If your feeder contains seed, it will attract seed eaters like finches and cardinals. If you offer **suet**, you might see insect eaters such as woodpeckers. And if you offer sugar water you might see nectar eaters such as hummingbirds. Not all birds found in your backyard are feeder birds. For example, a robin is a common backyard bird but it is rarely seen at a bird feeder because it likes worms and berries.

Below are photos of two of my favorite backyard birds. This pair of Eastern Bluebirds has lived in my backyard for three years. They use my nest boxes every year to raise new chicks.

Eastern Bluebird (6½"). Male has brilliant blue head, back, wings and tail. Female (above) is grayish blue. Feeds from perches, flying down to the ground to catch insects. Found in eastern U.S. Lives in farmlands, open woodlands, rural yards and my backyard! I nicknamed these two blue-birds "Dharma" and "Greg."

The following pages contain a collection of photos and information on feeder birds and other backyard birds to help you identify the birds you see. If you can't find your birds in this book, look in a field guide.

New Word?

Suet (SUE-it)

Animal fat. A mixture of animal fat and seeds or pieces of fruit that people feed to birds, especially in winter.

Time to Rise

By Robert Louis Stevenson from

A Child's Garden of Verses

A birdie with a yellow bill
Hopped upon my window sill,
Cocked his shining eye and said:
"Ain't you 'shamed, you sleepy-head!"

Stick Birds 1

You may notice that throughout this book many of my bird photos feature birds sitting on a stick. I call these birds my "stick birds." I like to photograph birds, so I tie a dead tree branch (one I found in the woods) to my deck near my bird feeders. As the birds come to eat at the feeder, they often stop on this stick just before or just after they get their food. When they do, I take their picture.

I take many pictures of birds on my stick. You can do this, too!

The 6" Tufted Titmouse (right) is mostly grey and white and has a crest and little button eyes. Males and females look alike. Titmice eat insects, seeds and berries and are common at feeders. They are found over much of the eastern U.S. in forests, city parks and suburbs.

The 5½" Chipping Sparrow (right) is a regular summer backyard bird throughout most of the U.S. It eats insects and seed on the ground and will visit feeders. Males and females look alike. In winter, its chestnut-colored crown is much duller than the summer crown seen here.

The 12" Mourning Dove (left) is one of the most reported birds at feeders. The male has light gray crown and iridescent sides of neck. The female is evenly brown on head and neck. They eat grass seed and grain seed and some insects and are found all over the U.S. in almost any open habitat.

The range of the 5" Black-capped Chickadee (left) is the northern half of the U.S. Its cousins include the Carolina, Mountain, Chestnut-backed and Boreal Chickadees, which all have specific ranges. Males and females of this species look alike. A friendly bird, it may eat from your hand if you are patient. It eats insects, seeds and berries.

The 6½" Downy Woodpecker (male shown left) works its way along tree trunks and branches, feeding on insects. Males have red on nape; no red on females. It lives in woods and suburbs and is found in the entire eastern half of the U.S.

The 13" Northern Flicker (male shown right) is common in parks, suburbs, farmlands and woodlands. The Yellow-shafted is found in the eastern U.S. Male has a black line off base of bill; female has no black line. The Red-shafted Flicker inhabits the western U.S. The male has a red line off base of bill, female none. It probes on the ground for ants and visits feeders for fruit, berries and seeds.

The 11" Northern Mockingbird (left) is found throughout most of the U.S. except the extreme northwest. The mockingbird mimics other songbirds. Males and females look alike. It eats insects, fruits and berries. It is is territorial during nesting season, and will chase away other mockingbirds, snakes, cats, large birds and even people!

Everyone recognizes the 10" American Robin (male shown right) whose arrival on lawns, meadows and golf courses in early spring marks the beginning of the season for many. Males have a darker head and chest than females. Robins eat earthworms, insects, fruit and berries.

Want some "stick birds" at your house? First, attract the birds by hanging feeders or place a handful of seed on your deck or patio or on the ground. Tie a tree branch on a fence or railing, high enough that no cat can get to it. It can take a few days for the birds to find the food. Then you can stand or sit about 10 feet from the food. Stay very still and the birds will eventually come to eat and perch on your stick.

Feed the Birds?

One of the best ways to see birds up close is at your feeders. Birds like water, too, for bathing and drinking.

To learn how to feed the birds, visit your local garden shop or wild bird store where you can find free information.

The 6" Tree Swallow (right) is another summer visitor to the northern half of the U.S. This cavity-nester builds a nest of grass, lined with feathers. Swallows eat insects, which they catch on the wing.

The 12" Common Grackle (right) travels in flocks and is very common east of the Rockies. Some Grackles have a purplish iridescence, others bronze. Males and females look alike but the female is less iridescent. Eats insects and seeds and occasionally other birds. Sometimes people mistake Common Grackles for American Crows, but the American Crow is much larger at 19". Other grackles found in different parts of the U.S. include Boat-tailed Grackles and Great-tailed Grackles.

The 7" Barn Swallow (left) builds a nest made of mud pellets. Both the male and female make hundreds of trips a day bringing mud to make the nest. Builds nest under bridges or on beams of big wood buildings, like barns. Nests are lined with feathers. Males and females look alike. Found all over the U.S. in the summer.

The 7" Cedar Waxwing (left) roams in flocks. Sometimes seen by the hundreds as they search for berries. Found throughout most of the U.S. Males and females look alike. Eats insects, wild fruits and berries. Its cousin the Bohemian Waxwing lives in the far northwest.

If You Find An Injured Bird

What do you do if you find an injured bird? It's often best to leave it alone. If a baby bird has fallen from the nest, you might be able to put it back in its nest. Otherwise, you should let nature take its course. I had to do just that a few summers ago.

In the second summer that "Dharma" and "Greg" nested in my yard, Greg was injured. I don't know how this happened but I couldn't believe how bad he looked when he showed up on my deck for mealworms. He was all wet and had broken feathers and a hole in his shoulder. I have no idea what happened to him.

Here's "Greg," the day after he was hurt (or attacked). His wing looked so bad I was surprised that he could fly.

This all took place during nesting season and Greg stopped feeding the babies for two days while he sat in a nearby tree to recover. He came for mealworms only two times in five days! Dharma took over all of the feeding chores. I was sad for him, but I could not interfere with nature.

Here's "Greg," about five weeks later with his feathers grown back and his injury healed. He looks as good as new again!

Poor Greg!

I think there is such a thing as too much birdwatching. One day, I was sitting on my deck with mealworms calling to my bluebird friend, "Greg." I always whistle so he knows the worms are ready for him and he always comes to eat. On this day I whistled and whistled but Greg didn't come. Through my binoculars, I looked for him among the trees where he often perches. No Greg. Finally, I looked down on the ground and there was Greg, on his stomach, wings spread out flat. "Oh no," I said aloud, "Greg is DEAD!"

I was in tears as I ran down the yard toward him. Just as I was about to kneel down to fetch poor dead Greg, he got up and flew away—just like that!

Later I learned that some birds like to sunbathe, just like humans do. Poor Greg, he wasn't injured at all! He was just enjoying his day—until I came running toward him like a crazy human. Like I said, sometimes you can watch a bird too much!

New Word?

Incubate (IN-kew-bate)

To keep at a correct temperature. Birds sit on their eggs to keep them from getting so hot or cold that the chicks inside them die.

Birdwatchers and Birdwatching

If you'd like to read stories about other backyard birdwatchers and their experiences watching and feeding birds, try this book:

The FeederWatcher's Guide to Bird Feeding

By Margaret A. Barker and Jack Griggs, published by Harper Collins. This book isn't written for kids, but it's not difficult to read. Here you can learn how to attract birds to your yard. You learn which seeds attract which birds. There are plenty of stories about backyard birding experiences, and they even tell you how they deal with squirrels and raccoons raiding their feeders. The book is based on real-life stories from members of Cornell's Project FeederWatch.

Finding nests is fun. It's easiest to find them in winter when the leaves are off the trees. But when nests are active in spring and summer, it's exciting to see the activity! During these seasons you can find nests by watching for parent birds flying to and from the nests. Once the eggs have hatched, the parents often spend a good part of the day bringing food to the nest.

Some birds nest on the ground, some in bushes, and some high in the trees. Some even nest in man-made things such as on top of porch lights or under raised decks. My neighbor found a bird's nest in the wreath she hung on her front door! For several weeks she and her husband avoided using the front door because they were afraid the baby birds would fall from the nest. Some birds, like woodpeckers and bluebirds, are cavity nesters—they build their nests in the holes of trees or in birdhouses.

Birds don't usually sleep in their nest during the daytime, so if you come across an adult bird in a nest, don't scare her off. It could be the mother incubating (in-KEW-bay-ting) her eggs. That's when she sits on the eggs to keep them warm so the chicks inside will develop. It's an important time for the growth of the chicks and they need the warmth of the parent's body.

If you discover eggs in a nest and no birds nearby, don't assume the nest is abandoned. Wild birds lay one egg per day until they've laid all of their eggs. Each species of bird lays a different number of eggs. They don't begin to *incubate* the eggs until the last egg is laid. So if you see eggs but no parents, the mother may not be finished laying her eggs. Carefully check this nest every day until the incubation starts. You might see an additional egg each time you do! But be careful not to disturb anything; don't touch the eggs and don't spend a lot of time near the eggs. You might scare Mom away permanently, and then the chicks will die for sure!

These baby Chickadees, hatched in one of our birdhouses, are only one day old and haven't opened their eyes yet. There's a picture of their Mom flying out of their nest box on every page of this book. Do you see her?

These baby tree swallows are only hours old. They are only as big as a thumbnail. I took this picture so you could see how small the babies are but you shouldn't touch baby birds or bother a nest in this way. A picture of their father is on page 24.

Do Not Disturb!

You should leave all bird nests undisturbed whenever you find them; summer, winter, spring or fall. Some birds will use the same nest next year and, if you remove a nest, you might be taking away a bird family's home! Besides, it's against the law to disturb a nest.

If you find an active nest with chicks or eggs, watch it from a distance or through binoculars. You can be sure the parents will stay nearby if you get too close to their nest. As you know, it's a parent's job to protect its children. If a parent bird is swooping close to your head or making a lot of noise at you, it means you're too close to its nest. Move away!

DO NOT DISTURB

Splish Splash!

Do you know that birds take baths? They do—to keep their feathers clean and free of dirt and tiny bugs so they can fly efficiently. Not surprised? Okay, do you know that some birds take dust baths?

Some birds—for example, blue jays—will smear ants through their feathers. This is called *anting*. Ornithologists believe that the ants may help to rid the bird of fleas and other tiny pests.

When your bird walk is over, there are a lot of fun ways to remain involved with the birds in your backyard. Here are a few examples:

✓ To attract more birds to your backyard, put up a bird feeder, birdbath or nest box. Consider hanging feeders from poles or purchasing a small feeder that sticks to your window with suction cups so you can see the birds up close.

✓ Start a life list to list the first time you see a new species of bird. Write where you saw it and when you saw it. You might include what the bird was doing such as flying overhead or perching on your bird feeder. Many birdwatchers keep life lists.

✓ Make your backyard into a place where birds would like to live. Birds (like all animals) need four basic things: food, water, places to hide and roost, and places to raise their chicks. If your yard provides those things, you'll have lots of birds around. If you set up your backyard right, you can even get it certified as a Backyard Wildlife Habitat. Wouldn't that be cool? To learn how to do it, check out the National Wildlife Federation Website at: **www.nwf.org**

✓ Join a Citizen Scientist program at Cornell University and help scientists study backyard birds. I highly recommend these programs for kids as well as adults! I belong to the Birdhouse Network and Project FeederWatch. See the sidebar on page 29 for more information.

✓ Join your local chapter of the Audubon Society. You'll help support our environment and you can join them for bird walks and seminars. To find your local chapter, visit the National Audubon Society at: *www.audubon.org.*

✓ Participate in a Christmas Bird Count (CBC), or the Great Backyard Bird Count, where you can help in the study of birds. Here, groups of birdwatchers count every bird they see within a defined area on a given day. Observations are reported to the National Audubon Society or Cornell Laboratory of Ornithology, which use the information to keep track of bird populations from year to year. Anyone can participate, even people who aren't expert bird observers. For information contact your local Audubon chapter or nature center, or visit this Website:
www.birdsource.org

If you like any of these ideas or you have some of your own, use the next page to write down your ideas so you won't forget to follow through with your plans.

You can also use the "My Ideas and Questions" on page 30 to write any questions that you thought of when you were on your walk today. Then later, when you find the answers to your questions, you can add them to your page.

I counted the birds at my local park during one CBC. There were a lot of Canada geese!

More about Birdhouse Network and FeederWatch Programs

To join a Citizen Science Program at Cornell you pay a small fee; and for that fee you receive lots of helpful information as well as a beautiful poster of feeder birds or cavity nesters.

In the Birdhouse Network, you place nest boxes in your yard (or, with permission, in a park) and you monitor the boxes throughout the nesting season, reporting your observations to Cornell at their Website. You report such things as whether or not your box is used by the birds, which species of bird, how many eggs are laid in the nest, how many hatch, and how many babies fledge (leave the nest). This project runs from the spring to the fall every year.

The Project FeederWatch program involves hanging bird feeders and then reporting which species of birds visit your feeders and how many individuals of those species you see at one time. You monitor the feeders once or twice a week for about an hour (monitoring time can vary). You report your findings to Cornell's Website. This project runs from November to April every year.

For more information visit:
birds.cornell.edu.

My Ideas and Questions

Need more room to draw or write? Use blank paper or download free forms at www.takeawalk.com.

Stop! And Start Again.

When you're ready to finish your walk, use the next page ("My Bird Walk") to complete your story and this book.

Write about your experiences today as you would write in a journal or diary. This will help you to remember the fun and interesting things you discovered during your walk. If you don't want to write a story, use the page to make a list of the birds you saw and identified today; you can start your life list right here!

Birdwatching is a wonderful hobby that you can pursue throughout your entire life, everywhere you go. If you enjoyed this walk, take it again and again because there's always something new to see. With your new knowledge and a good bird field guide, you can become an expert birdwatcher.

I hope you discovered lots of birds today. I especially hope that you found some birds you've never seen before. Today you became an observer of your environment. Because of this, you are now more aware of some good things in your world and you can now begin to change the bad things—even if it's something as simple as picking up the trash you see.

Thanks for joining me on this bird walk. Whenever you are outdoors, nature is around you. Keep observing. You can make great discoveries all year round—winter, spring, summer, and fall. When you don't have the time to take a nature walk, try a 20-Second Nature Break™. Twenty seconds is enough time to see something new. If you take a nature walk or a nature break every day, you'll see something new each and every day of your life!

See you in the outdoors!

Jane

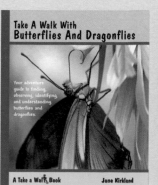

THE HOLDEN ARBORETUM

WARREN H. CORNING LIBRARY

9500 SPERRY ROAD

KIRTLAND, OH 44094-5172

DEMCO